S0-ADC-314

Noah
and the Ark

Cover illustration by
Michael Jaroszko

Story adaptation by
Sarah Toast

Interior illustrations by
Thomas Gianni

Interior art consultation by
David M. Howard, Jr., Ph.D.

Copyright © 1995 Publications International, Ltd.
All rights reserved. This book may not be reproduced or quoted in whole or in
part by mimeograph or any other printed or electronic means, or for presentation
on radio, television, videotape, or film without written
permission from

Louis Weber, C.E.O.
Publications International, Ltd.
7373 North Cicero Avenue
Lincolnwood, Illinois 60646

Permission is never granted for commercial purposes.

Manufactured in U.S.A.

8 7 6 5 4 3 2 1

ISBN: 0-7853-2222-1

PUBLICATIONS INTERNATIONAL, LTD.
Rainbow is a trademark of Publications International, Ltd.

There were many people on the earth in the years after God created Adam and Eve. But the people were very wicked. Their wickedness made God unhappy to have created people.

God decided that He must start all over again. He made up His mind that He would destroy all the people on the earth, and all the animals and birds, with a great flood.

But there was one good man on the earth. His name was Noah. Noah had a wife and three married sons.

God told Noah of His plan to flood the earth. Then He told how Noah and his family could be saved from the waters of the flood.

God instructed Noah to build a huge wooden boat called an ark. The ark had to have many rooms on three decks, and a door in its side.

Noah followed God's instructions. He worked very hard building the ark on dry land. At last he was finished building. The roof was very snug, and the ark was waterproof.

Then God told Noah to gather up two of every kind of animal and bird—a male and a female—to bring with him on the ark. Elephants and lizards, birds and ants, lions and gophers—every type of animal was brought together and placed on the huge ark.

It was Noah's job to keep all of the animals alive, so he had to find the right kinds of food for all of them and bring it onboard the ark. He also needed to have enough food for his wife, his three sons, and their wives.

After Noah had done all that God had commanded, God told Noah to go onto the ark with his wife and three sons and their wives.

God said, "In seven days I will send rain on the earth for forty days and forty nights." Every living creature of the land and air would drown except for Noah's family and the animals on the ark.

Noah and his family went onboard. The family members had rooms to live in, and the animals were comfortable in their stalls.

God shut the door of the ark. Seven days later, the rain started and began to flood the earth.

It rained without stopping for forty days and forty nights. At first the dry land became puddled, and the streams turned into gushing rivers. Then the floodwaters joined together and rose so that the land was covered with great lakes. The ark floated on the waters.

Then the waters swelled up even more and covered all the mountains of the earth.

Every animal, bird, and person died. Only those on the ark were left.

Even after the rain had stopped, the earth was still covered with water for one hundred and fifty days. At last the Lord made a wind blow. The wind began to dry up the great flood.

As the flood began to go down, the ark came to rest on top of a mountain. The mountain was called Ararat and was still underwater. Many weeks later, the highest mountaintops finally appeared above the water's surface.

One day Noah opened the window of the ark and sent out a dove. The dove couldn't find a place to land and returned to the ark.

Noah waited another seven days. Then he sent the dove out once again. This time the dove returned with a fresh olive leaf in her beak. That meant the waters must be going down!

One more week passed. This time, when Noah sent the dove out, she didn't come back. Noah knew then that the waters no longer covered all the land.

Noah removed the roof from the ark and looked out. He saw that the hills and mountains, valleys and plains, and even the rivers and lakes were just as they were before.

Then God told Noah and his family to leave the ark and bring all the animals out with them. The animals and birds all went out of the ark by families.

Every person and animal was filled with joy to set its feet on dry land again and to breathe the cool, fresh air outside of the ark.

The first thing Noah did was build an altar. He offered gifts to God to thank Him for saving his family.

Then God made a promise never again to destroy the earth with a flood. He promised that He would never again destroy every living creature, sparing only those on the ark.

God promised that, from then on, people could depend on a time to plant seed and a time to harvest, on heat and cold, summer and winter, day and night, so they could grow food for their families.

God set a beautiful rainbow in the sky as a sign of his promise never again to send a flood. God told Noah that when a rainbow appears in the clouds, it is a reminder of that promise.